D0323550

·THE LITTLE SCENTED LIBRARY·

FRAGRANT HERBS

·MALCOLM HILLIER·

SIMON & SCHUSTER
NEW YORK•LONDON•TORONTO•SYDNEY•TOKYO•SINGAPORE

A DORLING KINDERSLEY BOOK

SIMON AND SCHUSTER
SIMON & SCHUSTER BUILDING, ROCKEFELLER CENTER
1230 AVENUE OF THE AMERICAS, NEW YORK, NY 10020

FIRST PUBLISHED IN GREAT BRITAIN IN 1992
BY DORLING KINDERSLEY LIMITED,
9 HENRIETTA STREET, LONDON WC2E 8PS
PRINTED IN HONG KONG
10 9 8 7 6 5 4 3 2 1

LIBRARY OF CONGRESS CATALOGING-IN-PUBLICATION DATA
IS AVAILABLE ON REQUEST

INCLUDES INDEX

CONTENTS

INTRODUCTION

OVER THE LAST FEW years there has been a tremendous revival of interest in herbs. We are learning, once again, to appreciate the culinary and medicinal properties of herbs, and to savor their sweet, potent aromas.

The horticultural definition of herbs includes a wider group of plants than the layman's interpretation of the word. The term derives from the Latin, "herba a grass," which covers all plants that die down in winter. However, this is rather a broad use of the word, and we tend to think of herbs as plants with distinctive flavors or aromatic foliage.

Most common varieties of herbs can be grown in temperate climates, where the summers are warm and dry, and the winters are fairly mild. They are widely available in shops, but it is satisfying to create a small area devoted to herbs in a sunny corner of the garden, or grow them in containers on the balcony or patio. Whether you grow your own herbs or buy them from a shop, you can fill your home with their aromatic scents, concoct restorative potions and tonics for your skin and hair, and add an intriguing piquancy to your sweet and savory dishes.

FLOWERING HERBS

*M*ANY VARIETIES OF HERBS produce decorative flowers, which are also edible. Some are rather bitter to eat raw, but nasturtiums, chives, bergamot, and marigolds are quite delicious and make an attractive, colorful addition to salads.

Jerusalem sage *has gently aromatic leaves and flowers.*

Germander *has pink flowers with a spicy flavor.*

Nasturtium *is sweet, tangy, and colorful.*

Marjoram *has a sweet, aromatic flavor.*

Santolina *is tangy, and good for potpourri.*

Borage *flowers and stems have a cucumber taste.*

Blue-flowered sage has brilliant blue, bitter flowers.

Bergamot has a heavy, oriental perfume.

Chicory flowers are edible, and not too bitter.

Chive flowers taste and smell of onion.

Hyssop is aromatic, and is used in cooking.

Houttuynia has pungent, cream flowers.

Myrtle has delicate, honey-scented flowers.

Chamomile has pretty white flowers. Delicious in teas.

Marigold has a piquant taste and smell.

FOLIAGE HERBS

*A*ROMATIC LEAVES are widely used in cooking, and we are familiar with the flavors of many foliage herbs. Blended with scented flowers, these leaves can also add an intriguing fragrance to pot pourri mixtures.

Lemon verbena *has a glorious, tangy fragrance.*

Curry plant *has a curry scent and flavor.*

Chives *have a gentle onion flavor and are delicious in salads.*

Scented geranium *has a sharp, lemony tang.*

Spearmint *is good in ices, punches, and chocolates.*

Red ruffle, *or red basil, is a pungent but delicious salad herb.*

Lemon thyme *is highly aromatic.*

Sorrel *is spinach-like with a sharp, lemony tang. Good in soups.*

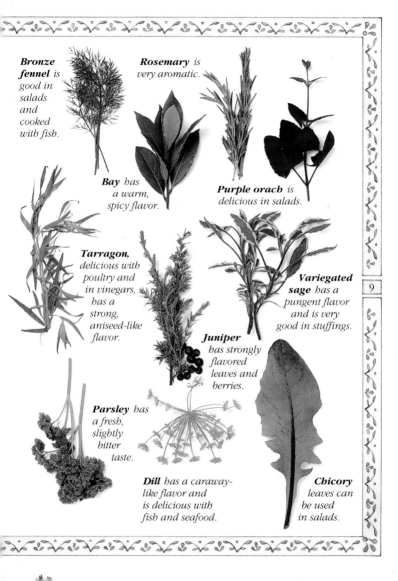

Bronze fennel is good in salads and cooked with fish.

Rosemary is very aromatic.

Bay has a warm, spicy flavor.

Purple orach is delicious in salads.

Tarragon, delicious with poultry and in vinegars, has a strong, aniseed-like flavor.

Variegated sage has a pungent flavor and is very good in stuffings.

Juniper has strongly flavored leaves and berries.

Parsley has a fresh, slightly bitter taste.

Dill has a caraway-like flavor and is delicious with fish and seafood.

Chicory leaves can be used in salads.

9

GROWING HERBS

OST HERBS can be easily grown in temperate climates, where summers are warm and the winters are not too severe. Herbs will flourish in the open soil, but I also like to grow them in pretty terracotta pots or other decorative containers. They can be placed in a light, sunny spot on the balcony, patio, or window-sill, or near the kitchen door, where they are fairly accessible. Their main requirements are plenty of light, a rich soil, good drainage, and sufficient water in the summer.

EVERGREEN HERBS
Bay, parsley, santolina, lemon-scented geranium, rosemary, and thyme form this decorative group of evergreen herbs. All of these are extremely aromatic, and are delicious used in cooking. Bay is wonderful with meat and fish, and its spicy tang also enhances the flavor of sweet milk puddings. Parsley is a perfect complement to fish, while santolina is often used in pot-pourris for its decorative and aromatic qualities. For any dishes containing lamb, veal, poultry, or game, I would suggest that you use either rosemary or thyme.

AROMATIC GARLANDS

*M*OST HERBS DRY QUITE EASILY and always look wonderful in decorative garlands. Dried herb garlands are fairly time consuming to make, but their natural beauty and delicious fragrance are well worth the time and effort. Hops are particularly attractive; they have a wild, rambling quality, a truly glorious aroma, and are also extremely simple to dry. Ensure that you hang your garland somewhere high and out of reach, as many dried herbs tend to disintegrate rather easily if you accidentally brush against them.

WILD HERB GARLAND

Fat bunches of garlic, brilliant red chilis, dried sage, dill, and flowering marjoram hang from a rope amid clusters of dried female hop flowers in this rustic, aromatic garland. It is stunning hanging on the wall and, if all the herbs are left undisturbed, it will last for many months.

POTIONS & TONICS

*O*VER THE PAST FEW YEARS there has been a revival of interest in the medicinal and therapeutic properties of herbs. Herbal potions, tonics, and aromatic tinctures are excellent cures for the common ailments that beset us all, such as headaches, indigestion, colds, influenza, and insomnia.

TINCTURE RECIPE
Soak 10 tbsp chopped fresh herbs or 5 tbsp dried herbs in 1pt (500ml) strong alcohol such as ethyl alcohol or vodka. Seal and store in a cool place. Shake daily for 2-3 weeks before use.

TINCTURE FOR TENSION
A chamomile and lavender tincture eases tension. Add 10 drops to a cup of warm water and drink at bedtime.

TINCTURE FOR HEADACHES
To relieve headaches, drink 5 drops of violet and thyme tincture in some warm water.

COLD SYRUP
For relief from colds and flu, take 2 tsp of dill and chamomile syrup. Dill aids sleep, and chamomile is a good decongestant.

ANISEED "DIGESTIF"
1 tsp of a peppermint and aniseed syrup prevents indigestion.

COUGH SYRUP
2 tsp of a syrup made from marsh mallow and coltsfoot eases dry coughs.

OIL RECIPE
Pour ½pt (300ml) good-quality vegetable oil onto 7 tbsp fresh chopped herbs, such as sorrel, chamomile, dill, and violets, and put the mixture into an airtight container. Leave in a warm, light position for at least 2 weeks before use. Shake the oil daily

SYRUP RECIPE
Pour 1pt (500ml) boiling water over 2 tbsp dried herbs. Allow the mixture to cool, then strain and place the liquid in a pan with 6 tbsp sugar. Heat gently until all the sugar has dissolved, then boil the mixture until the syrup thickens.

OIL FOR SORE THROATS
2 tsp of oil containing sorrel, violets, and honey will soothe an inflamed throat.

POTPOURRIS

*F*RAGRANT HERBS are one of the main ingredients of potpourris. Marjoram, rosemary, bay, mint, and lemon verbena all have highly aromatic leaves that complement the perfumes of flowers and add a warm piquancy to your fragrant mixes. To make potpourri, combine scented dried flower petals, dried herbs, spices, essential oils, and a fixative, such as powdered orris root. Store in a sealed jar for six weeks, and shake daily.

SUMMER-SCENTED BLEND
This potpourri of golden summer flowers is made from 1pt (500ml) part-dried marigold petals, 8floz (250ml) rose petals, 4floz (125ml) marsh mallow, 6 tbsp dill, 4 tbsp yarrow, and 2 tsp ground gum benzoin.

LAVENDER SCENTS

A fragrant cottage garden potpourri is made from 8floz (250ml) each of lavender flowers, sweet marjoram, and bergamot leaves, 4 drops bergamot oil, and 2 tsp powdered orris root.

ROSY MIX

This aromatic pot-pourri is made from a blend of 1pt (500ml) fragrant, part-dried rose petals, 8floz (250ml) rosemary leaves, 4 tbsp pink peppercorns, and 2 tsp powdered orris root.

FRAGRANT PILLOWS

*P*ILLOWS FILLED with herby potpourri mixes are a very decorative and enduring way to scent the house, as they exude a gentle fragrance, without ever exposing the potpourri to the air. Add about eight tablespoons of a light potpourri to the pillow stuffing, and enjoy its delicate, subtle perfume.

SPICY SCENTS
A decorative, thread-worked pillow in soft, muted blues, rusty pinks, and ochre, is filled with a spicy potpourri made from 8floz (250ml) scented mixed petals, 10 crushed cardamom pods, 2 tbsp crushed bay leaves, the grated peel of 2 oranges, and 1 tsp frankincense.

STRIPED PILLOW

An aromatic potpourri consisting of 4floz (125ml) each of fragrant rose petals and hop flowers, 4 tbsp sweet marjoram, the grated peel of 2 limes, and 1 tsp crushed tonka beans, is the perfumed filling for this very elegant, striped cotton pillow.

CHECKED COTTON PILLOW

This striking pillow exudes a suitably distinctive, tangy perfume. It is filled with a potpourri made from 8floz (250ml) lemon verbena leaves, 2 tbsp artemisia, 6 ground allspice seeds, and 2 tsp powdered orris root.

BEAUTY TREATMENTS

*A*ROMATIC HERBS are used in beauty preparations the world over. They are well known for their fragrance, as well as their cleansing, toning, and moisturizing properties. Make your own creams and lotions, and discover the herbs that best suit your skin type.

ROSE & ROSEMARY CLEANSER
Melt 2 tbsp lanolin with 2 tbsp beeswax. Add 2 tbsp each of warmed almond oil, warmed soy oil, and rose water, and 4 tbsp rosemary infusion. Beat until almost thickened, then add 7 drops each of rosemary oil and rose oil. For a rich color, add a small drop of red food dye if you wish.

ORANGE FLOWER & HONEY FACIAL SCRUB
For this scrub, melt 2 tbsp cocoa butter. Add 2 tbsp each of melted beeswax and warmed almond oil, and 1 tbsp pure honey. Stir in 2 tbsp each of ground rice and orange flower water, beat until almost thickened, and add 4 drops orange flower oil.

SAGE & LEMON ASTRINGENT

This piquant astringent is extremely refreshing and has a delicious, tangy fragrance. Soak 4 tbsp fresh sage leaves in 4 tbsp vodka and leave for a week, then stir in 2 tbsp lemon juice and 1 tbsp glycerine. Strain and store in an airtight bottle.

MOISTURIZER RECIPE

Melt 2 tbsp each of cocoa butter and lanolin, stirring constantly. Warm 5 tbsp of any fruit or flower oil and 1 tsp wheatgerm oil, and stir into the lanolin and cocoa butter mixture. Allow to cool until tepid, then add 3 tbsp of an herbal infusion with 1 tbsp glycerine and beat well. Store in an airtight container.

THYME & AVOCADO MOISTURIZER

A combination of avocado oil and thyme infusion makes an excellent toner and moisturizer for dry skin.

MARIGOLD & MARSH MALLOW MOISTURIZER

A marsh mallow infusion mixed with marigold oil makes a cream that gives your skin a healthy glow.

PERFUMED CANDLES

ANDLES CAST A WARM, flattering light in a room, and create an instantly intimate, romantic atmosphere. They can also be extremely fragrant, and fill the air with the delicate and intriguing perfumes of flowers and herbs. To make scented candles, you need only add a few small drops of essential oil to the melted wax during the candle-making process. I would suggest rose, thyme, lemon verbena, and rosemary oils for an herby aroma.

PRETTY POT
*An old flower
pot decorated
with a pretty ruff
of dried herbs makes an
attractive container for a
jasmine-scented candle. To
make the decorative ruff, I
simply glued aromatic dried
herbs in tiny overlapping bunches
onto the outer rim of the terracotta pot.*

OUTDOOR CANDLES

To make a fragrant outdoor candle, block the drainage hole of a flower pot, which is 4in (10cm) deep, with some clay. Attach a length of thick wick, 4in (10cm) long, to a skewer, and place the skewer across the top of the pot. Next, melt 1½lb (650g) paraffin in a small pan and heat to 160°F (70°C), stirring all the time. Add 5 drops of essential oil, such as lemon-scented geranium or rosemary. Pour the melted wax into the pot and leave it to cool. Cut the wick to ⅜in (1cm).

DECORATIVE CANDLES

Decorate a candle with dried flowers, such as marigolds and roses. To attach the flowers, warm a spoon handle over a flame. Place a petal on the candle and rub over it with the hot spoon handle. Repeat as necessary.

HERBAL DISPLAYS

A simple basket of dried herbs looks stunning hanging on the wall of your kitchen, living room, or hall. It can be highly decorative, and its fragrance should last for several months. I always think some of the most beautiful herbal arrangements are those that have a wild, unkempt appearance.

FRAGRANT BASKET

The basis for this very fragrant arrangement is a rustic half basket made of twigs and bracken. To make this display, wedge dry foam firmly into the cup area of your basket and stick small bunches of dried herbs into the foam. If you find the stalks of the herbs are not long enough, wire each bunch with a stout stub wire to give them an extended stem.

Using a mixture of foliage and flowering herbs gives the arrangement a glorious, muted range of colors. Here, I have combined sage, lavender, marjoram, rosemary, bronze and white fennel, tarragon, oregano, and goat's rue. As with all dried arrangements, it is best to hang this basket high up and out of reach to prevent it from being knocked. It is also important to keep dried herbs away from bright sunlight, so that they retain their colors.

Soaps & Waters

*S*CENTED SOAPS, bath salts, and waters have been made for centuries using purely natural ingredients. All of these toiletries are simple to prepare at home, and if put into pretty bottles, they can look very decorative arranged on the shelves in the bathroom or around the bath.

FRAGRANT WATER RECIPE
To make a refreshing toilet water, pour 1pt (500ml) boiling water onto 12 tbsp chopped fresh or 6 tbsp chopped dried herbs of your choice. When the water has cooled, strain the herb mixture and blend it with either 3floz (100ml) ethyl alcohol or 5floz (150ml) vodka. Add 10 drops of an aromatic essential oil. Store in an airtight bottle in a cool spot.

BAY WATER
For a refreshing skin splash, use crushed dried bay leaves blended with lemon oil, lemon geranium oil, and ethyl alcohol or vodka.

CHAMOMILE WATER
This makes a delicate, perfumed toilet water that will also act as a gentle skin cleanser. Combine chamomile flowers with bergamot oil, rose oil, and vodka.

ORANGE FLOWER WATER
The fragrance of orange blossom is captured in this blend of orange flowers and oil, and vodka.

MARIGOLD & PINE BATH SALTS
Pour 2lb (1kg) Epsom salts onto 7 tbsp fresh marigold petals. Add 12 drops pine or other aromatic oil. Store for 1 week, shaking daily before use.

SOAP RECIPE
Heat 2floz (75ml) of herbal infusion with 1floz (30ml) citrus juice and 5oz (125g) grated Castile soap. Allow to cool slightly, and add 1 tbsp each of chopped fresh herbs and oatmeal, and 5 drops essential oil. Mold, leave for 1 day, then wrap in tissue paper and leave for 4 weeks.

ROSEMARY SOAP
A scented soap contains rosemary and lime juice.

JASMINE SOAP
The heady scent of jasmine and the tangy zest of lemon juice are combined in this soap.

LINDEN SOAP
Make this soap by mixing linden flowers, grapefruit juice, and wallflower oil.

SCENTED SACHETS

*P*LACE SMALL SACHETS containing herbs, flowers, and spices in your drawers and wardrobes to impart a delicate fragrance to your clothes and ward off moths. To make these sweet bags, cut out a square of fabric, fill it with dried ingredients, and tie the bundle with a bow.

ROSE & ROSEMARY
A scented sachet that is perfect for the clothes drawer contains 3 tbsp each of rosemary and rose petals, and ½ tsp ground gum benzoin.

OREGANO & MINT
This sweet bag contains 3 tbsp each of oregano and mint leaves, and ½ tsp powdered orris root.

SANTOLINA SACHET

This aromatic sachet is also an excellent moth deterrent. It contains a mix of 3 tbsp each of santolina and perfumed mixed petals, and ½ tsp frankincense or powdered orris root.

LAVENDER & BERGAMOT

A fragrant bag for a closet or the linen cupboard is filled with 3 tbsp each of bergamot and lavender, and ½ tsp frankincense.

29

MARJORAM & THYME

This delightful hanging sachet contains 3 tbsp each of thyme and sweet marjoram, and ½ tsp oakmoss.

COOKING WITH HERBS

A ROUND THE WORLD, herbs are used to enhance the flavor of culinary dishes. In recent years, there has been a renewed interest in using a wide selection of aromatic leaves and flowers in the cooking of both sweet and savory dishes.

BOUQUET GARNI

A bouquet garni adds a distinctive flavor to soups, stews, and sauces. Wrap some aromatic herbs in muslin and secure firmly with string.

HERB BUTTERS

Breads, rolls, and crackers taste most delicious with these bold, colorful spreads. Simply blend a selection of finely chopped herbs, such as chives, tarragon, dill, nasturtium flowers, and sage, with a softened, good-quality butter, and chill.

HERB ROLLS

Sift 3 cups wholewheat flour and 2 tsp salt into a bowl, and add 4 tbsp chopped fresh herbs, such as chives, basil, parsley, or thyme. Heat 1 cup (250ml) water, 2 tsp sugar, and 1 tbsp olive oil until tepid and blend in 1 packet fresh yeast; add to the dry ingredients. Knead for 10 minutes. Leave to rise for 1 hour and knead again. Press dough into 16 greased muffin pans, cover, and leave for 20 minutes. Brush with egg yolk, herbs, and seeds. Bake at 400°F for 30 minutes.

HERBAL PRESERVES

*P*RESERVES OF ALL KINDS can be enhanced by the addition of aromatic herbs. These can liven up a bland jelly, temper the sharp astringency of a tangy, sour pickled preserve, or they can complement the flavors of sweet, fruity chutneys.

TOMATO CHUTNEY

Chop and fry 1lb (450g) onions and 3 garlic cloves. Stir in 1 tsp each of chili powder and ground cloves, and 2 tbsp dried mustard. Add 4lb (2kg) blanched, peeled and chopped tomatoes, 1¼ cups (350g) sugar, 1⅝ cups (400ml) wine vinegar, 30 chopped basil leaves, and salt; simmer for 50 minutes. Spoon into jars and cover. Leave for 2 months.

SWEET PICKLES

Peel and trim 4lb (2kg) firm vegetables (pickling onions, carrots, and peppers) and sprinkle with 4oz (100g) salt. Leave for 24 hours, then rinse and drain. Pack into jars, layering with sprigs of dill and some peppercorns. Heat and dissolve 4 tbsp sugar in 1 quart (1 liter) white wine vinegar. Allow the mixture to cool, then pour onto vegetables. Cover and store for 6 weeks.

APPLE PRESERVE

Heat and dissolve 1½lb (650g) sugar in 1 quart (1 liter) cider vinegar. Add 4lb (2kg) cooking apples (peeled and chopped), 2oz (50g) sliced fresh ginger, 1lb (450g) raisins, 10 sprigs rosemary, and 1 tbsp salt. Simmer until thickened. Spoon into jars and cover. Leave for 1 month.

MINT JELLY

Peel, core, and chop 2lb (900g) cooking apples. Put them in a large pot with 1¼ cups (300ml) each of water and wine vinegar, and the juice of 3 limes. Bring to boil and simmer until the apples are mushy. Strain this through a jelly bag and allow to drip for 2 hours. Pour the liquid into a pot and heat. Add 2lb (1kg) sugar and some lime peel; stir until the sugar has dissolved. Simmer until setting point. Add 1oz (25g) chopped mint and boil for 1 minute. Spoon into jars and cover. Green food colouring is optional.

SOUR PICKLES

Trim 4lb (2kg) vegetables, such as blanched and peeled whole tomatoes, cauliflower florets, and sweet red peppers. Sprinkle with 4oz (100g) salt, leave for 24 hours, rinse well, and then drain. Pack into jars and add some sprigs of tangy sage. Pour warmed, but not boiling, sherry vinegar over the vegetables until they are covered, and seal tightly. Store for 6 weeks.

ROSE CONSERVE

The perfumed taste of roses has been valued in the Middle East for centuries, where rose water is used to flavor sweets and pastries. To make this conserve, scald 1 quart (1 liter) fragrant rose petals in 1¼ cups (300ml) boiling water for 2 minutes. Squeeze through a sieve and discard the petals. Boil the rose water with the juice of 2 lemons, 1lb (450g) sugar (with added pectin to aid the setting process), and 2 cups (500ml) fresh rose petals, until setting point is reached. Spoon into jars and cover.

SUMMER PUNCHES

Q UENCHING FRUIT PUNCHES flavored with sweet herbs and garnished with edible flowers are quite delightful served at any summer party. Punches usually contain wine, and can occasionally be laced with spirits, but non-alcoholic ingredients, such as sparkling water, fruit juices, and tea, are extremely refreshing on a hot summer's day.

FRUITY MINT PUNCH
Heat 1 quart (1 liter) red grape juice with 4 tbsp sugar, until the sugar has dissolved. Add about 40 mint leaves and steep overnight. Strain the liquid, discarding the mint leaves, and add 1 quart (1 liter) each of red Côtes du Rhône and strong Earl Grey tea (made by steeping tea leaves in cold water overnight), and the juice of 3 lemons. Leave for at least 2 hours and decorate with an array of edible flowers, such as roses, nasturtiums, marigolds, primroses, pansies, borage, and violets.

OILS & VINEGARS

*H*ERB-FLAVORED OILS and vinegars add a
robust, distinctive flavor to many savory
dishes, including dressings, broths, stews,
and sauces. Create your own aromatic blends by steeping
herbs and spices in oils and vinegars to make really
delicious concoctions.

DILL VINEGAR
*This vinegar (right)
combines the light,
fresh flavors of dill
and anise. It is
delicious added to
sauces for fish and
salad dressings.*

JUNIPER VINEGAR
*Combine rosemary
with juniper seeds and
leaves in vinegar (far
right) to add a sharp
piquancy to rich beef
and game stews.*

ROSE VINEGAR

Rose petals and lemon-scented geranium leaves make a highly fragrant base for a dressing. Ensure that you select a light vinegar that will not dominate the delicate flavors of the flowers.

VINEGAR RECIPE

Crush the leaves and seed pods of your selected herbs and spices and cover in warmed wine vinegar. Marinate for 6 weeks. Use thyme, fennel, bay, and marjoram, or experiment with herbs and spices of your choice.

OIL RECIPE

To make fragrant oils, simply pour a delicately flavored, good-quality oil onto the fresh ingredients and leave to marinate for 6 weeks.

SPICY OIL

Season olive oil with herbs and spices such as peppercorns, thyme, rosemary, and chilies.

FESTIVE GARNISHES

G OOD FOOD TASTES all the more delicious if it is beautifully presented. A great variety of dishes can be enhanced by the addition of herbs and edible flowers, particularly if interesting color combinations are used. For a special celebration, garnish a mixed salad with flowers, decorate a pudding or cake with crystallized petals, or make an ice bowl encrusted with flowers and foliage, for filling with fresh fruit salad or ice cream.

DECORATIVE SALADS
Select vegetables of varying colors and shapes, such as lettuces, curly endives, peppers, and tomatoes, as the basis of your salad.

EDIBLE FLOWERS
Garnish your salad with colorful, edible flowers like these nasturtiums or violas.

MAKING AN ICE BOWL

Select two bowls, one 1in (2.5cm) larger than the other. Half fill the larger bowl with water and place the smaller bowl inside. Weigh the smaller one down with a metal weight, so that it floats. Secure with sticky tape, leaving ½in (2cm) gap at the bottom and the top. Push flowers and foliage down into the water, gently pushing them between the two bowls. Freeze and unmold the ice bowl in cold water.

FLORAL ICE BOWL

Serve your ice creams, fruit salads, chilled soups, and cool punches from decorative ice bowls. They are ideal for special occasions, and are impressive, yet really very simple to make. If they are returned to the freezer after use, they should last for several months.

SUGARED FLOWERS

Coat the petals or whole flowers of roses, primroses, fruit blossom, and pansies lightly with egg white. Using a strainer, sprinkle lightly with sugar, and leave to dry. The petals should last for a week.

INDEX

ACKNOWLEDGMENTS

The author would like to thank
Quentin Roake for all his help,
Rosemary Titterington of Idencroft Herbs
for supplying the herbs, and Osborne &
Little for the cushions.

Dorling Kindersley would like
to thank Pauline Bayne, Polly Boyd,
Gill Della Casa, Jillian Haines,
Mary-Clare Jerram, and
Caroline Webber.